PLUTO

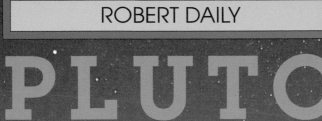

ROBERT DAILY

PLUTO

p

A FIRST BOOK
FRANKLIN WATTS
NEW YORK/CHICAGO/LONDON/TORONTO/SYDNEY

For Janet, as always

Cover photograph copyright © Astronomical Society of the Pacific

Photographs copyright ©: Don Dixon Spacescapes: pp. 8, 39, 51;
New York Public Library, Picture Collection: pp. 11, 14, 33, 36, 43;
The Lowell Observatory: pp. 16, 18, 19; North Wind Picture
Archives, Alfred, Me.: p. 21; The Hale Observatory: p. 25;
Astronomical Society of the Pacific: pp. 28, 45, 56; Finley Holiday
Film: pp. 30, 50; NASA/JPL: pp. 47, 55.

Library of Congress Cataloging-in-Publication Data

Daily, Robert.
    Pluto / by Robert Daily.
      p. cm. — (First book)
    Includes bibliographical references and index.
    ISBN 0-531-20166-X (lib. bdg.)—ISBN 0-531-15770-9 (pbk.)
    1. Pluto (Planet) — Juvenile literature. 1. Pluto (Planet)]
I. Title. II. Series.
QB701.D35   1994
523.4'82 — dc20   94-58   CIP   AC

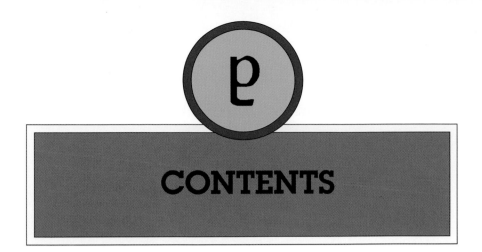

CONTENTS

CHAPTER 1
The Last Planet
7

CHAPTER 2
The Hunt for Planet X
10

CHAPTER 3
Pluto's Vital Stats
23

CHAPTER 4
A Frozen World
32

CHAPTER 5
The Double Planet
41

CHAPTER 6
Where Did Pluto Come From?
48

CHAPTER 7
Cannonball to Pluto
53

Fact Sheet on Pluto
58

Glossary
59

For Further Reading
61

Index
62

THE LAST PLANET

CHAPTER ONE

Until fairly recently, nobody even knew it was there!

Way, way out on the edge of the *solar system*, it floated in its weird and lonely orbit, a phantom ball of ice and rock—too far, too dark, and too small to be seen from Earth with the naked eye (or even most telescopes).

Even after it was "discovered" in 1930, this mystery object has kept its secrets well. With its crazy orbit around the sun—the strangest in the solar system—it's hard to pin down. It's even harder to spot in the sky. It is about 1,600 times too faint to be seen with the eye; through the largest, most powerful telescopes on Earth it shows up as only a tiny pinprick of light.

It may not look like it in this drawing, but Pluto (seen here with its moon Charon) is the oddball of our solar system — the coldest, smallest, and darkest planet.

What are we talking about? Pluto, of course—the last planet to be discovered, the last planet to be explored, and the last planet (we think) in the solar system.

The ninth planet from the sun, Pluto is truly the most unusual member of our solar family. It's a planet of extremes: not only the farthest planet from the sun, but also the smallest, coldest, and darkest planet in the solar system—and maybe the oddest.

It only makes sense that such an eerie, dark, and gloomy planet should be named after Pluto, the Greek god of the underworld.

Like the underworld, Pluto is a world unto itself. Remote, mysterious, and a long way from anywhere, it wasn't even discovered until this century—and then it took a certain amount of luck to find it. Today it's the solar system's final frontier, the only planet we Earthlings have not visited with a *probe* (a visit that is long overdue, and may happen soon). Still, in the last couple of decades, *astronomers* have learned a great deal about Pluto. Our picture of this mystery planet gets more detailed every year—and a fascinating picture it is!

Let's explore Pluto.

THE HUNT FOR PLANET X

CHAPTER TWO

For many years, astronomers played the part of planetary detectives. Finding clues was kind of tough, though—the object they were searching for was four billion miles away! The hunt for this mysterious, faraway body—the planet we now call Pluto—makes for an exciting yarn.

THE MYSTERY PLANET

For most of their time on Earth, human beings thought our solar family was made up of six planets, a few satellites, and a sun. Then, in 1781, British astronomer William Herschel

British astronomer William Herschel and his sister
Caroline scan the skies. Herschel discovered Uranus,
our solar system's seventh planet, in 1781.

found a seventh planet, called Uranus, floating about a billion miles (1.6 billion km) past Saturn. That, scientists decided, was where the solar system stopped. Or was it? Some astronomers looked at the unsteady course of Uranus and wondered.

Using formulas determined by Johannes Kepler and Isaac Newton, we can predict the *orbit* of a planet: where it will move and when. Scientists figured the orbit of Uranus, but whenever they looked for it in the sky, it would appear earlier or later than they predicted. So, they decided, there must be an unseen object out there whose gravity was tugging Uranus off course, making it go either faster or slower.

In 1845 a French mathematician, Urbain Leverrier, predicted (on paper) the existence of an eighth member of the solar system. The planet Neptune was then spotted in the sky a year later. But Neptune also failed to follow its predicted orbit. Why? There must be another planet out there whose gravity was pulling both Uranus and Neptune. Astronomers called this mystery object Planet X.

LOWELL: THE HUNT IS ON

One of the astronomers who noticed the slight changes in Neptune's orbit—and believed they were caused by a ninth planet—was a wealthy Bostonian named Percival Lowell. He used mathematical formulas to predict where this phantom object would appear at any given time. Then, in 1905, he started to scan the skies in search of Planet X.

Lowell believed so strongly in his prediction that he built his own Lowell Observatory. Flagstaff, Arizona, was the perfect place for this operation, offering a combination of dark skies and high altitudes to reduce distortion of telescope images caused by Earth's atmosphere.

Lowell searched long and hard for Planet X. Unfortunately, the telescopes of his day were not powerful enough to find such a dim, distant object. When he died in 1916, Planet X had not been found.

In 1929, Percival Lowell's brother donated money so the Lowell Observatory could build a new telescope. This instrument was especially designed for the Planet X search. It was a

Percival Lowell gazes at the heavens from his home near the Lowell Observatory in Arizona. His hard work paved the way for Clyde Tombaugh's discovery of Pluto.

wide-field telescope that could cover large areas and photograph thousands of stars in a single frame. With this state-of-the-art tool, the search continued.

TOMBAUGH: FROM THE FARM TO THE STARS

Many miles from Arizona, a young boy was doing some stargazing of his own. Born in 1906, Clyde Tombaugh grew up on a farm in Kansas, whose state motto is *Ad astra per aspera* ("To the stars through difficulties"). He was introduced to astronomy at age twelve by an uncle who had lent him a small telescope. Later he built his own telescope with some pine boards, leftover glass, and pieces of old farm equipment. He spent his days pitching hay and working the fields; his nights, scanning the skies and sketching the planets.

When Tombaugh was twenty-two, he sent his drawings to the Lowell Observatory. The astronomers there were so impressed that they offered him a position, even though he had no formal training. The job: looking for Planet X.

How do you hunt down a planet? It's not a very complicated process. You simply find a

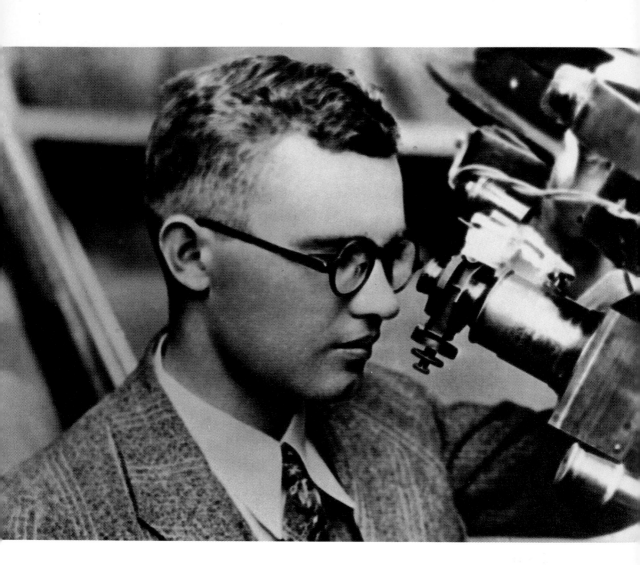

Clyde Tombaugh was only twenty-two when he left his Kansas farm for the Lowell Observatory. Less than two years later he made one of the greatest discoveries in the history of American astronomy.

tiny point of light in the sky and watch it for a few days. If it moves, it's probably a planet.

A simple task, yes, but a very grueling (not to mention boring) one as well. During the dark of the moon Tombaugh would take photographs through the Observatory's 13-inch (33-cm) telescope; during the day he would study the pictures. He was helped by a new invention that Percival Lowell didn't have—a "blink comparator." Developed in Germany, this instrument compares two photographs of the same area of the sky, taken a few days apart. It shows first one picture, then the other, moving quickly back and forth. As the images are compared, the stars will stay in the same position, but any object that moved during those few days will seem to "blink," or jump back and forth.

Tombaugh blinked plates for about a year. It was maddening work. In a single picture, he would have to carefully check as many as 35,000 stars! He had to ignore the dozens of asteroids that streaked across the photos. He also had to ignore the doubts of the people around him. One visiting astronomer told him: "Young man, I am afraid you are wasting your time. If there were any more planets to be

(Above) Clyde Tombaugh at the blink comparator,
searching for Planet X. Looking at photographs
taken six days apart (right), he noticed a speck of
light that moved. It was Pluto.

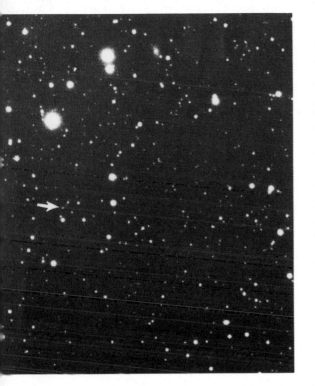

found, they would have been found long before this." But Tombaugh never quit.

Finally, on February 18, 1930, while comparing photos taken six days apart in January, Tombaugh noticed a dot of light that moved just a few millimeters. "That's it!" he shouted. He checked and rechecked his pictures before telling his bosses about his discovery. For forty-five minutes he was the only Earthling who knew that Planet X really did exist.

"There would never be another day like that one," Tombaugh later said. He was right. On an ordinary winter afternoon, a former Kansas farm boy added a ninth planet to our solar system, expanding the size of our universe by nearly 2 billion miles (3.2 billion km).

The last step was coming up with a name. Traditionally planets are named for figures from mythology, and many were suggested: Zeus, Cronus, Minerva. But the best suggestion came from an eleven-year-old English schoolgirl. She thought that such a dark, dismal planet should be named for the Greek god of the underworld. Also, the symbol for Pluto, ♇ , includes the initials of Percival Lowell, the man who started the search for Pluto.

What about Clyde Tombaugh? The only American to find a major planet went to college, where he wanted to take a beginning astronomy course. The professor wouldn't hear of it. "For a planet discoverer to enroll in a course of introductory astronomy," he said, "is unthinkable." Tombaugh later graduated and became a professor himself.

The darkest, most dreary planet was named for
Pluto, Greek god of the underworld. In this
drawing Pluto makes off with Persephone,
daughter of Zeus.

ANOTHER PLANET X?

Years after Tombaugh's discovery, scientists learned a surprising fact: Pluto was not big enough—it didn't have enough *mass*—to change the orbits of Uranus and Neptune. To have the predicted effect, Pluto would need to have about the same mass as Earth. We know today that it's only .002 times as massive as Earth.

So Pluto was not exactly the Planet X that Lowell, Tombaugh, and many others had searched for. In fact, it was a bit of a coincidence that Pluto was found where it was. At a later date, when the planet was in a different part of its orbit, it would have been far from the predicted spot. We certainly couldn't call the discovery of Pluto lucky, however, because it resulted from a lot of hard work by a great many people.

Is there a tenth planet out there? If so, it would be even farther from the sun than Pluto, and considerably more massive. Someday, perhaps, another young astronomy buff— maybe somebody reading this book—will make use of new technology to find the real Planet X.

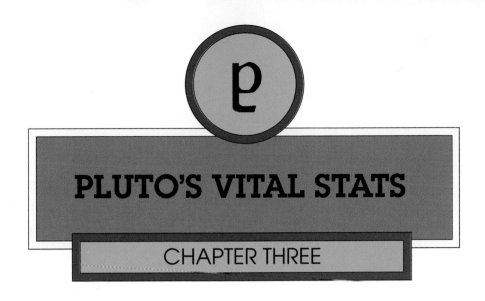

PLUTO'S VITAL STATS

How hard is it for us to see Pluto? Think of it this way: looking at the tiny, distant planet is about as easy as trying to spot a baseball from 100 miles (160 km) away!

There are a few reasons why Pluto is so hard to make out in the sky. The first is distance. Pluto is situated as many as 4.68 billion miles (7.53 billion km) from Earth. The second reason is faintness. The light we see reflected from Pluto has already traveled as far as 4.55 billion miles (7.32 billion km) from the sun, making the planet 1,600 times too faint to be seen with the naked eye. And any light that does make the long journey is distorted by the

Earth's atmosphere. Finally, making it even harder to see, Pluto is nearly lost in a background of numerous stars that are as bright or brighter than Pluto itself.

It's a wonder we know anything about this elusive planet. And, in fact, Pluto is too far away for us to make measurements that are perfectly accurate. But thanks to instruments that get better every year, scientists have learned a lot about Pluto's vital stats: its size, mass, density, orbit, and rotation.

THE INCREDIBLE SHRINKING PLANET

Since its discovery in 1930, Pluto has been shrinking! Well, the planet itself has not changed size, of course. But as our measurements have gotten more accurate, Pluto has gone from a giant to a planetary runt, not even as wide as the United States.

One of the first measurements of Pluto was made by a Dutch-American astronomer named Gerard Kuiper. He found its diameter, or width, to be about 3,725 miles (6,000 km). Later, some astronomers came to believe that Pluto was even larger, maybe closer to the

Even seen through a very powerful (200-inch) telescope, Pluto is only a faint spot, surrounded by many other spots of equal or greater brightness.

diameter of the Earth, which is 7,926 miles (12,756 km).

Soon after Pluto's moon Charon was found in 1978, scientists gathered a large amount of new information about Pluto. Once every 124 years, it seems, Charon's orbit reaches an angle so that we on Earth can see it pass directly in front of and behind Pluto. Fortunately, one of these rare eclipses happened in 1985, only seven years after Charon's discovery. Astronomers learned a lot about both planet and moon from this series of eclipses (as we'll learn in later chapters).

By timing Charon's trip across the face of Pluto, astronomers could measure the diameter of each. According to this estimate, Pluto is a mere 1,420 miles (2,290 km) across—only two-thirds the width of our moon, and about half the diameter of Mercury, which had been thought to be the smallest planet in the solar system.

These eclipses also helped scientists measure Pluto's mass (the amount of materials making up a body). According to the latest estimate, the mass of Pluto and Charon combined is only about 1/400 the mass of Earth. Pluto alone is only 1/6 the mass of our moon.

INSIDE PLUTO

Recently, the Hubble Space Telescope, an orbiting observatory launched by the space shuttle, gave astronomers a good look at Pluto without Earth's atmosphere getting in the way. They were able to get a good sense of the planet's *density*, or the compactness of its materials.

According to this study, Pluto's density is only about one-third that of Earth. The low density leads scientists to believe that Pluto is made up of equal amounts of rock and water ice. (Water has a lower density than rock.) They imagine that the heavier rock has settled to the planet's core. The *mantle* is mostly made up of ice, and the crust of methane ice (maybe mixed with other ices as well).

THE LONGEST YEAR

Without a doubt, Pluto has the oddest orbit in the solar system.

All the planets revolve around the sun with orbits that are *ellipses*, but most of these ellipses closely resemble circles. Pluto's ellipse,

however, is much more stretched out. At *aphelion*, or farthest distance from the sun, the planet is about 4.6 billion miles (7.4 billion km) away. At *perihelion*, its closest approach to the sun, Pluto is within 2.8 billion miles (4.5 billion km) of the sun.

In fact, Pluto can sometimes be closer to the sun than Neptune! Normally Neptune is the eighth planet from the sun. The shape of Pluto's orbit is so stretched, however, that for about 10 percent of the time, Pluto can actually be closer to the sun than Neptune. This odd little maneuver is happening now: from 1979 to 1999 Pluto will be closer to the sun than Neptune.

(Left) Way out in space, the orbiting Hubble Telescope gave astronomers a good look at Pluto without the distortions caused by Earth's atmosphere.

The tilt of Pluto's orbit is another oddity of the solar system. While the other eight planets orbit the sun in a flat plane, Pluto's orbit tilts away from this plane at a 17-degree angle.

Because Pluto is so far from the sun, one orbit takes a long, long time. A year on Pluto (the time it takes to make one revolution around the sun) is equal to 248 Earth years. People living on Pluto would never even reach their first birthday!

As for its rotation, Pluto takes a little more than 6 days and 9 hours to spin once on its axis. This period was determined by astronomers at the Lowell Observatory, who counted the days while dark splotches on Pluto's surface circled around and back again. The planet tilts on its axis at a 58-degree angle, which is about two and a half times Earth's tilt of 23 degrees.

(Left) Neptune is normally the eighth planet from the sun — but thanks to Pluto's stretched-out orbit, Pluto is actually closer to the sun about ten percent of the time.

A FROZEN WORLD

Any self-respecting planet watcher would give just about anything to spend a few hours on the surface of Pluto. (Or send a well-trained robot in his or her place!) Until that day, astronomers are learning all they can about Pluto's surface from the surface of our own faraway planet.

AN ICY SURFACE

Pluto is so small and distant that, even through the largest telescopes on Earth, it appears as a tiny point, without any distinguishable surface features.

Because Pluto is so far from Earth, astronomers must learn about its surface from Earth-based telescopes, like this one on Mount Palomar, California.

Since the 1950s, however, scientists have known that Pluto's surface is not uniformly dull. That was when they noticed that light coming from the planet was uneven: brighter in some spots, dimmer in others.

In 1976, using new infrared detectors that study sunlight reflected from Pluto's surface, they discovered that Pluto was coated with ice made mostly of frozen methane (though there's also some nitrogen and carbon monoxide ice). This ice is not distributed evenly across the surface, which is why Pluto's brightness seems to change.

Most of the ice is probably found at the planet's poles. As we learned earlier, Pluto's rotation is highly tilted. At any given moment, one pole is receiving direct light from the sun, while the other pole is partly shaded. So, while the planet orbits, the ice cap on the colder, shaded pole grows larger, advancing toward the *equator*; the ice cap on the sunny pole begins to melt, growing smaller. Both poles, however, stay covered with at least some methane frost throughout Pluto's 248-year rotation.

The far frontier of our solar system is a dirty place, with lots of dust particles floating around. Most ice turns muddy and dark out there in deep space. However, because the ice on Pluto is always melting and then refreezing, it stays clean and bright.

What would a map of Pluto's equator look like? That's hard to say. Aside from the polar regions, we don't know much about Pluto's surface. There are probably *craters* left over from ancient *meteoroid* collisions. Astronomers have noticed two large spots, one bright and one dark. They might be giant craters—maybe the bright one is filled with ice.

What about mountains or cliffs? Some scientists think that Pluto's surface ice is too soft and mushy to support such extensive features.

PLUTO'S ENVIRONMENT

Most planets are blanketed with an *atmosphere*, and Pluto is no exception—though it's a very, very thin blanket. A slice of Plutonian atmosphere (taken near ground level) would contain

This man-made crater was produced in a
NASA laboratory by a pretend meteorite.
Scientists believe that Pluto's surface
contains similar craters.

only about a thousandth as many gas molecules as a similar slice of Earth's atmosphere.

It wasn't until 1988 that we could be certain about this atmosphere. In that year, Pluto passed in front of a star in the constellation Virgo. Astronomers aboard an airborne observatory watched as the star's light grew slowly dimmer before disappearing behind Pluto, as if the star had been blotted out by the blanket of air surrounding the planet.

These astronomers noticed that Pluto's gaseous atmosphere has a clear upper level on top of a fuzzy lower layer. Because the planet's gravity is too weak to hold the gases close, they extend out as far as a couple of hundred miles—a long way for a planet that's only 1,420 miles (2,290 km) in diameter.

Infrared detectors tell us the atmosphere is made up of methane gas (along with nitrogen and possibly some argon or carbon monoxide). Isn't Pluto's surface also made of methane, in frozen form? Yes. Is this a coincidence? No.

In fact, the atmosphere is *created* when some of that surface ice melts and evaporates.

When Pluto (with its oddly shaped orbit) passes closer to the hot sun, more methane is evaporated, and the atmosphere gets thicker. Later, when the planet starts to travel away from the sun's warmth, some of that atmosphere freezes and falls back to the surface.

Thus Pluto grows a new "atmosphere" during one sweep of its orbit, only to lose that atmosphere a little later. No other planet in the solar system has such an unusual, ever-changing atmosphere.

By the way, when we talk about the sun's "warmth" hitting Pluto, that's a relative term! The coldest planet in the solar system boasts an average temperature of –395° F (–235° C). Imagine what a really cold day must be like!

THE BIG LEAP

Because Pluto is such a tiny planet, its field of gravity is very weak—only about 5 percent what we experience on Earth. If you weigh 100 pounds (45 kilograms) on Earth, you'd weigh a mere 5 pounds (2.3 kg) on Pluto. Think how high you could leap and how fast

Pluto at perihelion, when it is closest to the sun. "Close," however, is a relative term — even here the sun is 2.8 billion miles away!

you could run on such a planet! Each jump would be twenty times as high as on Earth.

What about a *magnetic field*? Well, Pluto is not only very small, it also has a very low density and it rotates very slowly. Large size, high density, and fast rotation are all conditions needed to generate magnetism. So scientists would be very surprised to find a magnetic field on Pluto.

THE DOUBLE PLANET

Astronomers devote their lives to learning about the planets. Hours spent glued to a telescope; long nights in the observatory, poring over photographs—it can be grueling work. But sometimes a little old-fashioned luck can be a scientist's best friend.

In 1978, an astronomer named James Christy was studying some photos of Pluto. (They were taken in Arizona, only a couple of miles from the site where Clyde Tombaugh made his discovery.) Christy was trying to study the planet's orbit, but he couldn't help noticing a bump that kept appearing on the side of Pluto.

This little lump, Christy determined, was moving; it was first on one side of Pluto, then the other. After examining the photos for a few more hours, he decided that the bump was in fact an orbiting satellite—a moon.

The new moon was named Charon, after the boatman in Greek mythology who ferried the souls of the dead across the River Styx to the underworld. (Pluto, remember, was Greek god of the underworld.) "Char" also happened to be the nickname of Christy's wife, Charlene.

DOUBLE YOUR PLEASURE

Because it wasn't discovered until 1978, scientists haven't had much time to study Charon. What do they know today about Pluto's only moon? Here are the basics.

Charon is about 740 miles (1,190 km) in diameter. This does not sound very big and, in fact, the state of Texas is wider. But Charon is more than half the size of Pluto, and nowhere in the solar system is there a moon so close in size to the planet it orbits. Our moon is the second largest, relatively speaking, and it is only about one-fourth the diameter of the Earth.

Pluto's moon was named after Charon, the mythological character who ferries the dead across the River Styx to the underworld (which was ruled by Pluto himself).

Charon almost seems too large to be a satellite of such a tiny planet. For this reason, scientists often think of Pluto and Charon as a "double planet." There's not another pair in the solar system like them.

THE DANCING PLANET

Charon orbits Pluto about once every 6 days and 9 hours. As you may recall, this is also the exact amount of time it takes Pluto to rotate once on its axis. The technical term for this is *synchronous rotation and revolution with mutual tidal coupling.* In other words, thanks to the forces of gravity exerted by each body, Pluto and Charon present the same sides to each other at all times. Like a pair of ballroom dancers, they are always facing one another. Once again, they are the only planet and moon in the solar system to behave in this odd way.

If you were standing on the surface of Pluto, what would Charon look like? First, Charon is either always seen or never seen, depending on which side of Pluto you're visiting. If you're on the proper side, the moon would never rise or set, but stay fixed in the same spot in the sky, as the sun and stars pass behind it.

Also, because Charon is only 11,650 miles (18,800 km) above Pluto's equator, it would look very large, about eight times bigger than our moon appears to us.

In this computer simulation, Pluto and Charon do their planetary waltz. You can see how steeply Charon's orbit is tilted.

One more thing about Charon's orbit: as seen from Earth, it is tilted very steeply, at a 58-degree angle. This is why we only see it "eclipse" (pass in front of and behind) Pluto for one 6-year span every 124 years. As we noted earlier, it is through these rare eclipses that we have learned so much about Pluto's vital stats. If it wasn't for James Christy's lucky discovery, Pluto would still be a mystery.

ANOTHER FROZEN WORLD

Little is known about Charon's surface. It is probably uneven, and pockmarked with craters. Also, scientists think it is covered with ice, like Pluto; but instead of methane ice, Charon is believed to be coated with ordinary water ice.

Why would two heavenly bodies so close together have different surfaces? As the smaller of the two, Charon has a weaker gravity field, too weak to hold on to any methane gas. So methane has escaped from Charon's surface, leaving behind the layer of water ice.

As you can see from this artist's conception,
Pluto's moon is quite large compared to Pluto
itself — more than half as big, in fact.

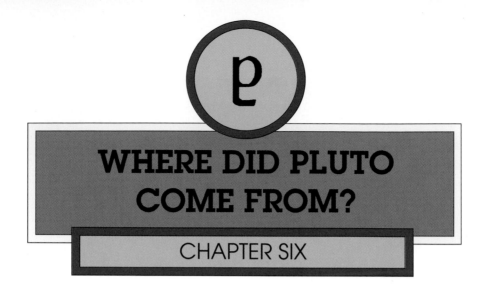

WHERE DID PLUTO COME FROM?

CHAPTER SIX

As we've seen again and again, Pluto is the oddball of the solar system. And in one other area, its composition (what it's made of), Pluto definitely fits into its own category. It's not one of the "terrestrial" planets, those inner planets of the solar system (Mercury, Venus, Earth, Mars), which are mostly made of rock. Nor is it like its neighbors, the outer planets (Jupiter, Saturn, Uranus, Neptune), which are basically balls of gas.

So how did this unusual planet come to be formed?

RUNAWAY MOON?

A few decades ago, a popular answer to that question was what we might call the "runaway moon" theory.

In 1956, astronomer Gerard Kuiper said his studies proved that Pluto was an escaped satellite of Neptune, Pluto's neighbor. According to Kuiper, Pluto once orbited alongside Triton, a moon of Neptune, until something—maybe a near collision with a passing star, or with Triton itself—caused it to escape Neptune's gravity and take on its own orbit around the sun.

It's true that Pluto is quite similar to Triton. They're almost the same size and density (both are mostly made of rock), and their atmospheres are equally thin. But astronomers now believe there's another explanation for these similarities.

According to the latest theory, both Triton and Pluto are leftover "planetesimals." Some five billion years ago, when our solar system was born, there were many such objects—chunks of rock and ice—that formed from a gigantic cloud of dust and gas. For a while they drifted around the young sun. Over time, however, some of the objects started clumping

(Above) Triton, a moon of Neptune, is very similar to
Pluto in terms of size and density. Astronomers think
that both Pluto and Triton were "planetesimals"
created during the birth of our solar system (right).

together to form the giant outer planets.
Others were ejected from the solar system or
flung into the sun to burn.

Some were captured by the larger planets,
with their greater mass and stronger gravity,
and turned into moons. Triton, for example,
was captured by Neptune soon after its birth.

And one lost little planetesimal was left to
wander in its bizarre orbit. That's right: Pluto.

PLUTO'S IDENTITY CRISIS

Pluto is so small, and so much like Neptune's moon Triton, that some astronomers have wondered, Is it even a planet?

The answer is yes. For one thing, Pluto moves in a predictable orbit around the sun. So do comets and asteroids, the so-called minor planets, but Pluto is twice the size of even the biggest asteroid. In fact, Pluto has three times as much mass as all the asteroids in the solar system combined. Also, unlike any asteroid, Pluto has enough mass and gravity to hold onto a satellite (Charon) and an atmosphere.

By almost any definition, Pluto is a planet. An odd, unusual planet, but a planet just the same.

CANNONBALL TO PLUTO

Poor Pluto! The smallest, coldest, farthest, oddest planet in our solar system is also the least popular: the only one that hasn't been explored by Earthlings.

For years, scientists have been asking the National Aeronautics and Space Administration (NASA) to send an exploratory spacecraft (unmanned, of course) to this final frontier. For years, they have been disappointed. In the 1970s, before *Voyager 2* was launched to study the five outer planets, a Pluto encounter was cut during final planning because there wasn't enough money.

So Pluto still hides its secrets from the eyes of scientists. But its luck may be changing in the next decade. NASA has proposed sending a probe, called the Pluto Fast Flyby, that would get within 6,000 miles (9,700 km) of the far-away planet's surface!

Actually, the Pluto Fast Flyby will consist of two probes that will leave Earth a year apart; if one runs into trouble, the other can serve as a backup. Each spacecraft will be equipped with a camera, an infrared and an ultraviolet spectrometer (instruments that analyze the sunlight reflected off Pluto's surface), and a radio transmitter to relay the data back to Earth.

Weighing less than 250 pounds (115 kg) (compared to one ton [0.9 metric ton] for *Voyager 2*), they will be light and compact, the better to make the 4-billion-mile (6-million-km) journey. One NASA scientist describes each probe as like a cannonball carrying a camera and a radio.

The Fast Flyby is well named; the probes will be so speedy that they'll fly by Pluto in only about an hour. But a lot of information can be gathered in that time. Also, the cameras will start snapping pictures six months

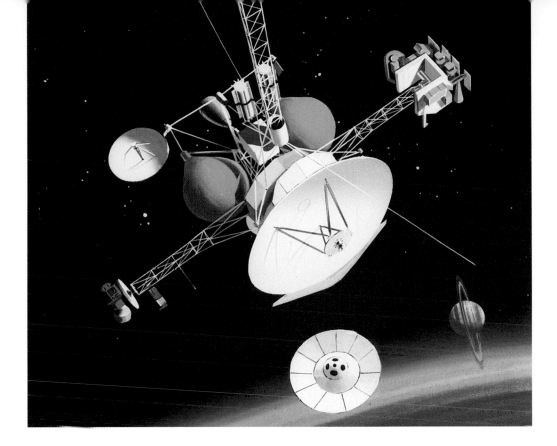

The Voyager 2 spacecraft explored Pluto's neighbors in the 1970s. Pluto is the only planet that has never been explored by a probe.

before the probes make their close encounter. These cameras are so powerful that even from 6,000 miles (9,700 km) away they can see objects that are only a half-mile (0.8 km) across.

There's only one hitch. The Flyby has to leave soon (before the end of the century) if we want

The rings of Neptune.
Scientists wonder if
Pluto, Neptune's
neighbor, might
have a similar ring.

to learn about Pluto's atmosphere. After that time, Pluto will begin to leave the sun's warming rays, and the planet's atmosphere will freeze and fall to the surface.

The Pluto Fast Flyby will greatly increase our knowledge of the phantom planet. Astronomers will finally get answers to questions they have been asking for decades. Does Pluto have another moon—or several other moons—that our telescopes cannot spot? Does it have a ring, like its neighbors Uranus and Neptune? Is its surface flat and boring, or is it varied like Earth's?

Once these questions are answered, we will be rewriting all the books about Pluto. According to one NASA scientist, "There is only one thing of which I'm certain about the Pluto encounter—and that is that we'll be surprised by what we find."

One last note about the Flyby. When NASA decided to send the probe to Pluto, they called Clyde Tombaugh, then eighty-six years old, and asked for permission to visit "his" planet. The professor said sure. He jokingly warned them, however, that it would be a "long, cold trip!"

FACT SHEET ON PLUTO

Symbol for Pluto — ♇ . The symbol is made from the letters P and L, after Percival Lowell, whose work led to Pluto's discovery.

Position—in average distance, Pluto is the ninth and farthest planet from the sun. Its nearest neighbor is Neptune.

Rotation period—it takes Pluto 6.3872 Earth days to rotate once on its axis.

Length of year—one year on Pluto (the time it takes to travel once around the sun) is 247.7 Earth years long.

Temperature—the average temperature on Pluto's surface is –395° F (–235° C).

Diameter—about 1,420 miles (2,290 km).

Distance from the sun (depending on location in orbit)—closest, or perihelion: 2.75 billion miles (4.43 billion km); farthest, or aphelion: 4.55 billion miles (7.32 billion km).

Distance from the Earth (depending on orbit)—least: 2.66 billion miles (4.28 billion km); greatest: 4.68 billion miles (7.53 billion km).

Number of moons—one, named Charon. It is 740 miles (1,190 km) in diameter and is located an average distance of 11,870 miles (19,100 km) above Pluto's equator.

GLOSSARY

aphelion—the point in a planet's orbit where it is farthest from the sun.

astronomer—a scientist who studies the universe beyond Earth.

atmosphere—the various gases that surround a heavenly body.

axis—the imaginary line through a planet's core, around which it rotates.

core —the innermost part of a planet.

crater—a bowl-shaped hole in a planet's surface, caused by the impact of a meteoroid.

crust—the outermost layer of a planet.

density—the compactness of materials.

equator—the imaginary line that circles a planet around the center.

gravitational field—the area around a planet in which an unseen force pulls objects toward the planet's center.

magnetic field—the area around a planet in which a compass needle points to the magnetic north pole.

mantle—the middle layer of a planet, between its core and crust.

mass—the amount of matter in an object.

meteoroid—a flying body made of stone or metal.

orbit—the curved path of an object circling another object.

perihelion—a planet's closest approach to the sun.

probe—an unmanned spacecraft sent to study a planet or heavenly body.

solar system—our sun and all the objects that revolve around it, including the nine planets, their moons, comets, meteoroids, and asteroids.

FOR FURTHER READING

Asimov, Isaac. *How Did We Find Out About Pluto?* New York: Walker, 1991.

Asimov, Isaac. *Pluto: A Double Planet.* Milwaukee: Garth Stevens, 1990.

Asimov, Isaac. *Saturn and Beyond.* New York: Lothrop, Lee & Shepard, 1979.

Brewer, Duncan. *The Outer Planets.* New York: Marshall Cavendish, 1992.

Davis, Don. *The Distant Planets.* New York: Facts on File, 1989.

Fradin, Dennis B. *Pluto.* Chicago, Ill.: Childrens Press, 1989.

Littman, Mark. *Planets Beyond: Discovering the Outer Solar System.* New York: John Wiley & Sons, 1988.

Tombaugh, Clyde W., and Patrick Moore. *Out of the Darkness: The Planet Pluto.* Harrisburg, Pa.: Stackpole Books, 1980.

INDEX

Italicized page numbers
indicate illustrations.

Aphelion, 29
Asteroids, 52
Astronomers, 9, 10, 12–24, 37,
    41, 49, 57
Atmosphere, 35–38, 49, 57

Blink comparator, 17, *18*

Charon, 26, 42–*43*, 44, *45*, 46
Christy, James, 41–42
Comets, 52
Craters, 35, *36*
Cronus, 20

Density, 24, 27
Discovery of Pluto, 7, 9, 12–22,
    24
Distance, 23–24

Earth, 22–24, 26, 27, 31, 32, 46,
    48
Eclipses, 26, 46

Ellipses, 27
Environment, 35–38, 57
Equator, 34, 35, 44
Exploration of Pluto, 53–57

Faintness, 23
Formation of Pluto, 48–52

Gravity, 12, 37, 38, 44, 46, 49,
    52
Greek mythology, 9, 20, 42

Hale telescope, *33*
Hershel, William, 10, *11*, 12
Hubble Space Telescope, 27,
    28

Ice, 32, 34, 35, 46, 49

Jupiter, 48

Kepler, Johannes, 12
Kuiper, Gerard, 24, 49

Leverrier, Urbain, 12

Lowell, Percival, 13, *14*, 17, 20
Lowell Observatory, 13, 15, 17, 31

Magnetic field, 40
Mantle, 27
Mars, 48
Mass, 22, 24, 26, 52
Mercury, 26, 48
Meteroids, 35
Methane, 37
Minerva, 20
Moon of Pluto, 26, 42–43, 44, *45*, 46, 57

National Aeronautics and Space Administration (NASA), 53, 54, 57
Neptune, 12, 13, 22, 29, *30*, 48, 49, 51, *56*
Newton, Isaac, 12

Orbit of Pluto, 24, 26, 27–31, 41

Perihelion, 29, *39*
Pluto, *8, 19, 21, 25,39, 45, 47*
    density of, 24, 27
    discovery of, 7, 9, 12–22, 24
    environment of, 35–38, 57
    exploration of, 53–57
    formation of, 48–52
    mass of, 22-26, 52

moon of, 26, 42–43, 44, *45*, 46, 57
    orbit of, 24, 26, 27–31, 41
    rotation of, 24, 31, 34, 44
    size of, 9, 22, 24, 26, 52
    surface of, 32–35, *36*
Pluto (god), 9, 20, 42
Pluto Fast Flyby, 54–55, 57
Probes, 9, 54–55, 57

Rotation, 24, 31, 34, 44

Saturn, 12, 48
Size of Pluto, 9, 22, 24, 26, 52
Solar system, 7, 9, 12, 20, 25, 31, 35, 42, 48, 49, *51*
Sun, 9, 10, 23, 27, 29, 31, 38, 49, 52, 57
Surface of Pluto, 32–35, *36*

Telescopes, 7, *12*, 13, 15, *16*, 17, *27, 28, 32, 33*, 41
Tombaugh, Clyde, 15, *16, 17, 18*, 19–20, 22, 57
Triton, 49, *50*, 51, 52

Uranus, 12, 22, 48

Venus, 48
Voyager 2, 53, 54, *55*

Zeus, 20

ABOUT THE AUTHOR

Robert Daily received a B.A. in English literature from Carleton College and a master's degree in English literature from the University of Chicago. He is a magazine writer for both adults and children and is also the author of *Mercury, Earth,* and *The Sun* in the First Book series. He lives with his wife, Janet, in Chicago.